M000198522

salmonpoetry

Publishing Irish & International
Poetry Since 1981

Keeping Planes in the Air
Lori Desrosiers

This collection is published in 2020 by
Salmon Poetry, Cliffs of Moher, County Clare, Ireland
www.salmonpoetry.com   email: info@salmonpoetry.com

Copyright © Lori Desrosiers, 2020

ISBN 978-1-912561-87-2

All rights reserved. No part of this publication may be reproduced
or transmitted in any form or by any means, electronic or
mechanical, including photography, recording, or any information
storage or retrieval system, without permission in writing from the
publisher. The book is sold subject to the condition that it shall not,
by way of trade or otherwise, be lent, resold or otherwise circulated
without the publisher's prior consent in any form of binding or
cover other than that in which it is published and without a similar
condition, including this condition, being imposed on the
subsequent purchaser.

Cover Design & Typesetting: *Siobhán Hutson*
Printed in Ireland by Sprint Print

Acknowledgments

"About the Body" won the Liakoura Prize from Glass Lyre Press. Published in *Skin Deep* anthology, 2018

"Ferry" in *We Are Beat, National Beat Poetry Festival Anthology 2019* from Gems Press.

"I See my Grandmother Bella's Face" in The Worcester Review, Vol. 38, November 2017.

"Google Search for my Parents' First House," "Ceremony," "Beth with Hummingbirds," "Words are not Enough" and "Before the Split" in *Peacock Journal*, July 23, 2017

"How Small" and "Mother on the Beach" in *Writing in a Woman's Voice*, July 2017

"Forgetting" was a finalist for Amherst Live poetry prize

"For Gary" in *First Literary Review East*

"Elephant of Mortality" on Split this Rock's blog

"Blur" in *Pirene's Fountain* 10th anniversary issue

"The King of Television" on Nicholas Kristoff's Blog in *The New York Times*

"I Dream of the Bus to Hell" and "Since I'm Awake Listening to You Snore in the Other Room" in *Alexandria Quarterly Review*

"For Now" in *New Verse News*, April 4, 2017

"At the Tea Tasting" in *Pirene's Fountain*

"Praise to the Earth" in *Carrying the Branch*, an anthology for world peace from Glass Lyre Press

"Found" in *The Valley Advocate* article: *Selected Poems from the Mass Poetry Festival*

"The Last Fall" in *The Mom Egg*, Volume 15.

"Salt" in *Blue Lyra Review*

"Boy on the Train" published as part of "Stuck in the Atlanta Airport" in *Nixes Mate Review*

Contents

Presence & Absence

Bodies & Dreams

Spaces & Possibilities

Presence
&
Absence

Google maps search for my parents' first house

No more mailbox, no number
the woods a tangle of brush
and stone, fallen down steps,
driveway overgrown, cracked.

The entire top of the hill razed
sand and silt, no trees
below hollowed out house
not even ours.

Ours is gone, torn down
maybe even before the heat
of our bodies had faded
on divorce's road to other lives.

Behind the house where grapes
grew on trestles, now some sort
of huge hole in the ground
foundation for a stadium
or some kind of quarry, hard to tell.

What is gone is where we grew
snapdragons and peas, irises
zucchinis, there were bees
a picture window with ivy
baby robins in a nest
hornets on slate rock patio.

We had a clear view of the Hudson
above apple and pear trees
blossoming crabapple and cherry
paths in the woods, rocks to climb

A massive tulip tree, yellow flowers
thick branches, home to so many birds
trunk blackened by lightning,
one of the first cut down.

The hill was so steep my mother
feared taking the car down,
yet down we went.

Before the split

barefoot summer days
daffodil's white spring bloom
long grass white pulp chewed
cling of cotton shorts sweat
plucked stripped yellow flowers
toes scooped wet stones
pocketed pink quartz
surveyed caterpillars' climb
sting of rain dazzle of lightning
not yet phased by future

dallied in creek water
airborne by breath
feet met soil rocks ants
bees caressed honeysuckle
sipped sweetest part
practiced skimming flat ones
caught newts tadpoles toads
up oak birch maple bark
scudded home daisies bending
not yet split asunder

Benevolent Ghosts

Writing a book of ghosts,
I consider whether I believe.
Nevertheless they are here.

My father's spectral hand
pushing me towards
the man I loved and kept.

Beethoven on the breeze
or blue herons in flight
bring needed comfort.

On the road driving once
a hawk swooped down
looked me straight in the eye.

Cab drivers after Japan's tsunami
carried spectral passengers who disappeared
leaving only the fare on the meter.

My grandmother hovered
before my mother's car on her way
to my grandfather's deathbed.

Perhaps spirits are less mysterious
than we think they are.
If I believe anything, it is
there are benevolent ghosts
who linger, reach out, watch over.

My mother teases she'll haunt me
when she's gone. I'm sure she will.
Her voice is already in my head.

Famous Last Words

When Grandpa Jack was dying
my mother, speeding down
the New Jersey Turnpike
to be at her father's side,
swears she saw the ghost
of Grandma Bella
flying across the road,
beckoning her to hurry.

She reached the hospital
spent time with her father
then left the room.
Grandpa must have thought
he was still in Russia, or perhaps
was angry at the doctors
for letting him die.
His last words were
Come the revolution, I'll get you!

My Grandmother Shoplifted

She loved pearls, even fake ones
big bracelets of gold fabric, clip-on earrings
anything shiny, woven, lush.

When my grandmother walked into the five & dime
the fake jewelry called her to its shelves
where she caressed each glass ring, each bracelet

then put them in her purse, her pocket
or her brassiere. Soon she had bureau drawers
filled with baubles, and she wore them

every day, until the day, age 70
they arrested her, but put her on probation,
due to her advanced age, the low value of the goods.

She gave back a pile, hid the rest under her delicates.
Grandpa packed her up and moved to the suburbs
so she couldn't walk to Woolworth's anymore.

I See my Grandmother Bella's Face

Lately in the mirror I see
not my mother's face
but my grandmother's.

Not her green eyes
but my brown, reflecting hers
behind our almond lids.

Her cheeks sag as I age
and when I don't smile
but purse my lips

and stretch
my head up
to tighten our hanging neck

she looks back at me,
her white hair still thick
styled nearly the same.

I expect her to speak to me
in her Russian accent
to call me *Lorela*.

Garlic

Of all that comes with aging,
I didn't expect my mother
to have forgotten
her table manners.
We pass the roasted garlic
around the restaurant table
at her 90th birthday celebration.
She sees it and exclaims
Oh, look, garlic! takes her spoon
proceeds to eat it from the bowl.
My brother whispers
I guess we're not getting any.

Ghosts of Sohoku (found poem)

(after the 2011 Tsunami, Japan)

"I learned that the death of each victim carries importance."

Yuka Kudo Sociology Student, Tohoko Gakuin University

I.

After the tsunami
taxi drivers picked up ghosts
of young people
distraught
lost perhaps.
A woman in a coat in summer
asked to go to Minimihana district
The driver told her the area was empty.
Have I died?
Voice from the back seat.
The driver turned to look
she wasn't there.

2.

It is suggested the dead may have chosen taxis
because they need a private room
to process bitterness at their deaths.
Take me to Hyoriyama
The driver saw him
pointing to the mountain
through the rearview mirror.
when they arrived
he was gone
the tick of the meter
the only proof.

3.

Lined up at a shop
that used to be there
old and young
some headless, limbless.
The woman who sees them
calls the exorcist.

Writing in Emily Dickinson's Bedroom

They give me a pencil
so as not to stain
her room with ink.

How does the presence
of hundreds of visitors
stain her cherished privacy?

Would she sigh at
each clack of footsteps
on the stairs?

Her washing bowl
blue and white
porcelain for ablutions

where she washed off
soot from the stove
or ink from her fingers.

Quill on her writing table
an inkwell, empty
no ink allowed
even for a ghost.

the ghost of our intentions

when what we meant
hides behind what we say
when the parental dictum
it's not what you say
it's what you do
confounds the tongue
when every time we speak
the burden of composition
follows the flap of lip
despite our best efforts
to make speech rational
and the ghost of our intentions
lingers in peripheral vision
like the flash of light
from a torn retina

In a certain light

for Monica Hand

Late at night
when I can no longer
do math
my words
fold
into images
of friends lost
to time's slippage.

Then
I think of you
and even though
it has been so long
since I saw you last
there you are
in a certain light
and I am comforted

by the thin veil
of real permanence
of how we used to sit
watch the bowl of stars
circle around us
of how we knew
we would always
be.

I Am Not

I am not
the missing mother
the lost child
a forgotten song
the one abandoned
the second one married
the closet where you put me
the dirt on your shoe
the first notch on your rifle.

What I am
started over
the moment I
walked away.

Mother on the Beach

Our young mother in her navy blue bathing suit
cream cheese sandwiches on the beach.

My brother's nose under white cream
Mother kept him covered on the beach.

Mother carried a wicker basket
or was it a metal cooler, on the beach.

She would hold a towel for my brother
so he could change his shorts on the beach.

He had freckles and I didn't
My pale little brother on the beach.

Before I die, I'd like to see the ocean again.
She's too old, too frail to get to the beach.

We'd run into the churning surf, if it could
carry us back to Mother on the beach.

Ferry

The great doors lift
the keening sea
churns and roars.
Darkness between you and the dock
calling you down
then you wake.
Night world
of ferries and carousels
cotton candy towers rising
wondrous and terrifying
almost as bad
as the real ferry
from Woods Hole to
Martha's Vineyard
when you were six
waiting with your parents
helpless in the line of cars
as the metal ramp
came down what seemed
inches from crushing
swallowing cars
like a wide mouthed tunnel.
No child could have conjured
a scarier monster.
Even on board
soft pretzels proved
of little comfort
only to nap
and fall again
into gaping darkness

Keeping Planes in the Air

Keeping planes in the air was my mother's job.
She believed in the power of worry, and prayed
every time I traveled by air. Since she turned 90,
we have stopped telling her where we are going.
The worrying makes her ill, so I have taken on the job.

My daughter and unborn grandchild are in the air.
She is flying to Paris with her friend Laura for a week.
The problem with doubting the existence of a god
is no longer feeling in control of things with prayer.
My daughter will have time to contemplate
while nursing her little one next spring; how the bridges
across the Seine were lit and Notre Dame
stood touching its gothic towers to the sky.
Today I implored whoever might hear my voice
to bring her there and safely back to us,
while trying not to imagine what happens
when a plane crashes into the sea.
Her husband is waiting for her to come home.
Meanwhile I track the plane on my computer,
say a prayer to the spirits that protect us both,
and worry just enough to keep the plane in the air.

De Milo

She would have held him
if she had arms I'm sure of it
the lover she gazes at all day
from her marble eyes.

Perhaps she would hold a leaf
in her hands or a flower
to give to a passing child
staring up at her torso.

Even armless she is lovely
after all she is a goddess.

Does she mourn the break
remember her trauma and weep
when the museum guests
have left the room?

Joe on the Beach

for Joe Gouveia

Joe is a huge heart poet.
He tells me don't listen
to people who aren't Joe.
Joe has my best interest.

Joe finds joy in places
you and I never look.
He pushes aside boulders
welcomes the worms to light.

Joe died in the early spring.
He sits on the beach and waits.
We all think he's gone
but he's right here in our hearts.

Forgetting

Little by little, as I watch my mother's mind decline
I am losing hold of my own sharp focus.
My usual ability to keep the balls in the air
wanes. I drop a couple here or there, run after them.
These small forgettings, blind spots
in my usual clear-sightedness frustrate and annoy me.
So I go along and make more lists than usual
then forget to look at them.
Visiting my mother reminds me
that she is on a slope now.
Some days are clearer than others.
She starts to tell a good story, then we come to a gap.
The year she took me to the opera, she has forgotten.
Some of the stories have changed dates, times.
People are switching roles, names.
The more I try to put aside the fear of my mother's death,
the more I see her hand coming out my sleeve.

Books for my Mother

My mother read *War and Peace*
encouraged me to do the same
and I did, with a pencil and paper

to keep track of all the characters
all 1296 pages worth.
Now she inspects a book I brought.

This one is so long! What is it about?
I tell her the premise again.
I thought she might like this one.

I had given her a shorter book
for her birthday in October,
but she read a couple pages

and put it down.
She asks me for books,
says she's bored in the evening.

I forget that she forgets,
can't recall what she just read.
Still, the pile grows by her chair.

Side-effect of short-term memory loss

you dream memories now
the one where you drive across the Tappan Zee
and a man in a car follows you
so you turn into the Irvington police station

or the one where you are dancing with Walter
even though he's your friend's husband
and you don't kiss him
because you don't want to

or the one where you are visiting Jane down in
Shank's Village in New Jersey where you first met
and you fall in love with her little girl Ellen
whose name is my middle name

you can't remember anything new
whether you took your insulin
where your husband is

when he goes to the doctor
or the store
or the other room

My Mother Dreams (a ghazal)

My mother calls me in the morning
says she thought I was in Martha's Vineyard

In the morning she is fog and storm
both my mother and Martha's Vineyard

I rode my first horse her name was Buffy
my father was alive in Martha's Vineyard

The sea rose and ate the beach
eroded clay cliffs in Martha's Vineyard

I walked with my brother on a rock jetty
Mother was not afraid on Martha's Vineyard

Where are you, Lori, are you there?
My mother dreamed I was in Martha's Vineyard

My Heart

after a poem of the same name by Kim Addonizio

(For my parents)

That hot dog with mustard from a cart
on the corner of 79th and West End Avenue.

The metal swings in Riverside Park.
The tall, narrow windows in the dancer's studio.

The crowns on the bridge to Queens
with cars backed up, honking.

The street vendors' wares piled high on their blankets
knock-off purses and watches spilling onto the sidewalk.

The pigeon shit on every windowsill.

That apartment, that shouting, that pillow of loss.
That bookcase you filled. That country house you fled.

That trip you never took again. That city you loved
where you were young and together

imagining your future
imagining me.

The Last Fall

Cleaning the blood from the kitchen floor
when my stepfather fell and broke two ribs
red seems to be everywhere.

Paper towel it up, she insists
Or you'll have to clean the mop.

My hands shake,
uncomfortable
too close to the source.

I make myself hibiscus tea
briefly forgetting the color
pour it down the sink.

We eat in the kitchen
I wonder where it splattered,
were these mats on the table?

I empty the garbage, there are
bloody gauze pads in the recycling.
I bag it all and put it out.

The room where I sleep has red wallpaper
a painting with red flecks
a red and orange batik of a fish.

I am here to save her from worry.
When she naps, I nap.
At least I do not dream in red.

Asleep in her recliner
her mouth turns down at the sides.
Does my face do that?

Her husband has fallen
Fifteen times this year alone
my mother twice.

If the next fall is his last
she will be too broken
to save.

For Blanche

I miss you while you're still here
    your voice is my voice with a Philly accent

we both speak French and learned to sing art songs
    I write poetry, you wrote two novels

your hair used to be thick like mine
    now it's thin and so white

you ask the same question four times
    in the course of a phone call

I call to keep you alive
    you answer to find out if anyone still loves you

How Small

How small is your world, Mother.
Each day you wake, slowly.
The aide gets your breakfast,
always two poached eggs,
orange juice, decaf coffee
and rye toast. You never want
to get dressed, prefer to sit
for hours in your recliner
in red bathrobe and blanket.
You look at the New York Times
even though you no longer retain
what you read. The days I come
to take you out we have to argue.
You say, *I am too tired, I can't do this.*

If I could, I would not disturb,
not force you out of your chair.
Are you afraid, my mother who
traveled, who wrote, who sang?
Daughter of Russian Jewish
immigrants, who survived
poverty, the depression, two wars,
who worked, raised her children
alone after divorce, how is it
you still look beautiful at 93?
In your little world, you fall
asleep sitting in your chair.

Bodies
&
Dreams

A Dream

I left babies in various places
in a box,
in a stroller,
in a tree.
Always the same baby
multiplied.
I think they may be poems
I have not written.

For Gary

I wish you were more of an optimist
I wish you wanted to install solar, plant vegetables,
let violets overrun the lawn,
march against racism, go out to a movie.

I wish you would drink less, lose the belly
take walks with me, write with me.
I wish you liked poetry more, could sing,
had more money. Okay no that's not true.
I wish you were just you in my dreams.

Wake Up Call

The days before were quiet
interrupted only by the idea of cataclysm.
First line of a student's essay:

I've been shot before, but this time was different.

Last year he was walking to his car, BANG.
It didn't hurt as much as last time
He thought it was maybe fireworks, or a ball from a BB gun.

The next day upon waking
he couldn't feel his leg.
His brother carried him to the car.

He's quiet, a freshman in my Composition class
has an easy smile and now
permanent fragments from a 22.

Each day I wake, work, go home
retreat from the untenable curtain of media
turn off the news in hope it might be fiction.

Another student says she's seen people shot.
Several others nod.
Oh miss, it happens all the time, we're used to it.

Since I'm awake listening to you snore in the other room

Your face is smooth like a child's when you are sleeping
or in a coma
The chaplain in training at the hospital thought you were
my son
I told her you were my husband and she was
embarrassed
The nurse told you a long story about ice fishing and I
asked her why
Since they put you in hypothermia you needed something
to dream about
I watch you sleep sometimes now amazed at your unimpaired
breathing
No buzz of machines, just the pellet stove's even hum
your asthma mostly at bay
You are used to my asking if you are okay are you sure
are you sure

Triangle Shirtwaist Factory Fire

March 26, 1911

No one knows how the fire started.

Sixteen-year-old
Frieda sings Schubert's
"Die Forelle"
while she sews.

Her dress caught on a wire,

"So fängt er die Forelle
Mit seiner Angel nicht."
"I saw the small trout playing
within the crystal brook."

the crowd watched her hang there

Lise, Maria and Esther
change their shoes,
pin their hats,
watch the clock.

till her dress burned free

Treadles: wooden, rhythmic,
painful through thin slippers
worn on the long walk
from Europe to New York.

and she came toppling down.

"Und ich mit regem Blute
Sah die Betrogene an."
"And I, alas, downhearted
must see the victim caught"

> *"Is it a man or a woman?" asked the reporter.*
> *"It's human, that's all you can tell," answered the policeman.*

NOTES:

Italics from the NY Times article of March 27, 1911.

Song lyrics are from Franz Schubert's "Die Forelle (The Trout)"

My grandmother was not in this fire, but she worked in the garment district for a year
around the same time period. The women in the photographs looked just like her.

Playing Bach's Brandenburg Concerto in High School Orchestra

From the back of the violin section
practice was grueling:
one measure at a time
we scribbled finger positions
chewed the broken pencils
Mr. H. threw at us
when we played wrong notes.

At first we were twenty different
violins playing separately
only the first row, the seniors, in tune.

"You sound like a High School orchestra!" shouted Mr. H.

So we practiced
and we practiced.

My cheap student violin squeaked
high on the E and mother's wail
Must you do that when we're here?
made it worse.

But after a week, or two, or ten
the strings began to resonate together
first violins in tune
second violins, almost.

"Much better!" bellowed Mr. H.

And we played
and we played
until our chins were scarred and our fingers bled
and the Brandenburg
stayed in our heads forever.

Rewind Sonata

Don't forget me don't forget me

She is still here but not.
Who is this when I show her
photographs of her great grandson.

The grief chord repeats…

I want to play it all backwards
put her at her piano

me underneath, listening
to her vivacious soprano
singing Shubert *lieder*.

about the body

how the house we carry with us changes,
what it feels like to see
the face age, how the breasts fall
how pain becomes a given
how the skin was once unblemished
and smooth, like the curve
of earth or sunbeams bent by trees
it is also about caves
the ones we dig to hide secrets
a wish to get beyond mirrors
how my mother is shrinking
she says she'll end up
a puddle in the kitchen
no one will recognize
this poem is about emerging
about finding beauty in imperfection
how skin stretches to accommodate
bones their restless march towards death.

Sofia's Thumb

for Sofia Zanzarella, PT

Odd how pain rises
in the nerves, wakes
the brain at night.

Muscles grip
cleave to the bone.
In daylight, my body

twists, contorts
stone to the touch.
Doctor signs a pad

sends me driving, hunched over
up a flight of stairs
holding the rail.

With her thumb
Sofia pushes
starts slow, then it hurts.

Sometimes I scream, swear
but as quickly as it came,
release.

Freed from bone's tug
nerves relax
muscles and mind

I exhale a long-held,
long-awaited
breath.

The Reason to Love a Bridge

The reason to love a bridge
is you are on the other bank
always a river away
an estuary for my poems

The bridge aches with foot traffic
everyone is longing for you
or a version of you
the saddest ones leave footprints

Fishermen cast their lines
over the bridge's side
they keen as poles lean out
reaching but not attaining

Beneath the bridge the water
casts aside our longings
goes about its business
of getting to the sea

Elephant of Mortality

I hear another military jet
whining overhead and the
only elephant in the room is
the wooden one on the
coffee table. or it could be
when I check on my mother
every night, or listen for the
next shoe to drop, or the
clock in its blatant forward
motion, our mortality
humming like feedback from
a speaker marking the
moment, which is all there is,
so I watch the gray cat pull
and push her breath, listen to
my husband snoring as I type
each night, when insomnia
begs me to hold onto the last
possible second of today, in
case of a hiccup in the
continuum, in case, for
someone I love, tomorrow
never comes.

Redemption

At midnight I notice
the stretch between time zones.
Hawaii eats last night's supper while
Ireland is waking to tomorrow.

We live unaware of the curvature of Earth
undaunted by atmospheric shift
unfazed by sunspots, tidal currents.
Meteors pass, satellites hum
we sleep unconcerned.

We are a blip
someone once said
in the arc of history
and what we call history
is only the human story.

We look for evidence
of ourselves in our world's soil
but before that were millions
of years without us
after us is forever time
beyond even the concept of time.

Yet there are good things
legends we have invented,
stories told, art wrought
songs sung for centuries
evidence of our best selves.

Despite our future slumber
in time's uncaring cradle
this is our hope for redemption.

The birds are more resilient than we are

The birds are more resilient than we are.
winter snows and ice heave the soil
this year nearly devastated the trees
where herons nest above the flood plain.
Somehow, they find new trees in which to roost.

Today I saw a red-tail hawk in hunting mode,
in flight, wings back, talons extended.
There are more hawks, crows
small birds migrating north, waking us
at dawn when we are torn
between staying put and taking flight.

Ferry Ride with Lines from Whitman

Riding the ferry from Bridgeport to Port Jefferson
I think of you, Walt Whitman, how you stood
at Brooklyn's Wharf, contemplated the multitude
of immigrants who rode these waters.

The glories strung like beads on my smallest sights and hearings,
on the walk in the street and the passage over the river,

You watched how the water turned from dark to lighter blue,
flowed over deep channels and races filled with schooling bluefish.
Boats, baited with nets and hooks, waited for men
to set out from the city where we both were born.

Others will enter the gates of the ferry and cross from shore to shore,
Others will watch the run of the flood-tide,

One hundred fifty years after you wrote,
immigrants still pour into New York Harbor
where Lazarus' poem is beginning to fade
from the plaque at the statue's feet.

What is it then between us?
What is the count of the scores or hundreds of years between us?

Some of us today believe in your America.
We believe that without diversity, this harbor will be
nothing but shallows, un-navigable, bereft of poetry.

Flow on, river! flow with the flood-tide, and ebb with the ebb-tide!
Frolic on, crested and scallop-edg'd waves!

Ice Fishing in the ICU

*Therapeutic hypothermia…refers to deliberate
reduction of the core body temperature in patients
who don't regain consciousness after return of
spontaneous circulation following a cardiac arrest.*

–www.americannursetoday.com

The nurse shivers as she works
despite her down coat.
Bare hands check
my husband's breathing tube
the respirator's click and hum.
She replaces an ice pack under his arm,
hangs a new bag of Propofol.
She seems to be talking as she
smiles at me through the glass
then opens the door to let me in.
I want to hold his hand
but am not allowed to touch.
It will be thirty hours
before they can wake him.
*I was telling him a story about
ice fishing,* she says.
Something to dream about.

Blur

used to be a photograph
colors faded by water
human-shaped

who took this
from whose house
is it still there

were they able to salvage
the walls, did they tear out
the sheetrock, the wood floors

the soaked carpet
the children's blocks
floating out the door

pots and a toaster
bouncing on water
like a tiny boat parade

which flood did this
and did the people
in the photo survive

The King of Television

All hail the king of television
Gaimon's book come true
the gods of materialism have won.

He walks onto the stage
framed by a giant screen
cameras strobe in applause.

Phones held high light the Mall
the hired audience sings an ode
to whiteness, money, success.

Someone punches in the code
fake fireworks light the Memorial
Pretend to remember Lincoln

pretend to remember King
pretend to admire Obama
pretend to care about history.

He doesn't care to care
he thanks you all for coming
but you are not there.

You are at the protests
lighting candles
waiting, watching

for his inevitable fall
as five letter signs
tumble to the pavement

We are real, there are more of us
and we know how to switch
the televisions off.

My Name is Light / Vigil for Orlando

light light, my name is light Lenora
the one my parents gave but never called me
from the Arabic *nur* meaning light
my candle one of the first ones lit
I wander and find myself lighting candles
looking in each person's eyes
do you need some light I asked
gay and lesbian, bi and trans, queer
of all colors, shoulder to shoulder
listening and waving,
raising fists and candles
light has to be our future
no more violence no more hate
has to, because if it is not
our lights our pulse our names
the ones our parents gave us
the ones we call ourselves
will become extinguished

I Dream of the Bus to Hell

Propelling down a metal road
steep as the escalator at the
Toys R Us in Queens
where I had to ride backwards
to quell my nausea.

With vacant eyes, riders stare
don't rise, but I do.
There is a demon driving
muscled and formidable,
barreled chested, pumped
beneath gray suit and vest.

I climb onto a passenger,
stand on his shoulders
he doesn't even notice.
I push on the ceiling and
a tile comes loose.
My head pokes through
but something tugs at my feet.

City Girl in the Suburbs

She feels the electric lips of dark
does not sleep but notices
the rumble of a cat near her head

white underbelly pulsing
its body blocking the digital clock.
She looks again and an hour has passed.

Her partner snores, his breath shallow,
his hand heavy by her shoulder,
his presence calms her.

It is summer, cicadas all night,
and when birds awaken him at 5am
he threatens to get his BB gun, but doesn't.

This is a quiet street,
unlike the city where she used to live,
where the constant hum of engines

steam rising from underground ducts,
men, women shouting from windows,
honking cars, and lights

invaded every window, reflected on buildings,
their post-neon urban charge
flashing advertisements.

For Now

I look out my window
and it is not raining acid
my street is not flooded from erosion
the air is not filled with smog
the herons who fish from the nearby river
are alive and the trout are plentiful
honeybees drink from backyard honeysuckle
gardens grow rich with zucchini and new tomatoes
an hour away the ocean is swimmable
the astounding thing is
with one signature
the rain, the air, the soil, the fish
the birds, the flowers, the bees,
the water, and we humans,
not slowly, but quickly
perish

Spaces
&
Possibilities

Ceremony

(response to prayers for Standing Rock)

when drum
        and singing
                resurrect
                        a heat
stirs
        beneath your
                thick shell
                        cracking
long-piled
        protections
                at least
                        momentarily
and you wait
        for this
                to cede
                        but are driven
                                skyward
well at least
        your thoughts

and you lose
        the fear
                you wear
                        and join in.

Rooted

Late night, pellet stove hums,
white noise becomes white space

dancing on the currents
blowing by my chair

which is dark wood
better than cheap pine.

There used to be a marble table
now the old wooden coffee table

your father made,
has several plants on it.

I only know the names of two,
Norfolk pine and Christmas cactus.

There used to be an ivy hanging,
it dwindled to stem and a few leaves,

so you put cuttings in water to root.
I asked today if it was rooted yet

you said, it takes a long time
to develop roots.

It took me years to find you
and this place to come home to

where I feel at peace.
We have rooted like the ivy.

There are Leaves

after an early snowstorm
leaning into November
there are leaves
and there are bare branches
perhaps they are dead or
the snow dropped them
or peak color is past
or fall came too soon
sumac and red maples
still red, some brown
patches of brown
yellow on oak, hickory
soon they'll all be bare
but for now
there are leaves

Neighbor

Baldwin, NY 1982

My ex grew corn
in the tiny back yard
just a couple stalks,
also peas, tomatoes,
basil, rosemary,
pumpkins, squash.
The time we left
for a few days,
an elderly Chinese man
from down the street
had found our garden,
and we found him
on his knees
pulling weeds.
He stood, as if
he thought we
might be angry.
We thanked him,
told him to please
come back anytime.
He beamed.

Mother and Apple Pie

I know, I wasn't much of a cook.

Mother never made brisket
or homemade matzo balls
or pretty much anything except
baked chicken or turkey.
She would put an onion inside
for flavor and I still do that, so
she cooked a little, I guess
also roast beef. Maybe
she just didn't like brisket.
Once she made apple pie
from her Settlement Cookbook
and she says it was pretty good.
At ninety-three she claims she
made apple pie several times
but I only remember the one.

Boy on the train

Past midnight at the Atlanta airport, a young man is on the train that travels between gates. When we exit, he does too, but he does not follow us up the escalator. I see him play with the zipper on his back pack, and head back to the train. I know what he is doing. He is as lost as the rest of us, not knowing what to do to pass the time until morning when our planes leave, unable to get a hotel, or not able to afford one, so he's riding the train, back and forth, from Baggage Claim to Gate D. He is in the one warm spot at the airport. Settling near our gate for the night, I know he is still there, pretending not to ride the train.

At the Tea Tasting

Wielding egg-blue teapot, refilling our cups
she discussed the proper way to steep tea.

Don't boil the water like the English
and don't milk the tea, she explained,
that's the way to burn
the leaves and dull the flavor.

We tasted Oolong from China,
Chai from India and spiced fruity
Rooibos scented with vanilla and cinnamon,
Green teas from Sri Lanka and Japan,
from light and sweet to dark and bitter,
organic Assam and Darjeeling blacks,
Earl Grey, Ginger and Coconut.

Did you know you can decaffeinate
your own tea by simply steeping twice?

She thanked us and gave us each
a small bag: a gift of Darjeeling leaves.
Now to resist the urge to milk the tea.

stepped into the music store
and fell in love

rosin and horsehair dark wood
flecked black from years of use
a cigarette burn ashes dropped
he must have smoked while playing
the old man who played this violin
I hear Hungarian dances not fiddle
bowing almost effortless my body
knows without having to think
tone better than my student violin
a German Stradivarius copy
well-loved but not coddled
fingers on my left hand reach for notes
my music comes back to me

The Homage Stitch

The Persian rug maker
leaves a stitch undone
a purposeful imperfection.
The Navajo weaver
adds one bead or stitch
of a different color to a rug
to release its spirit.

Are we capable of perfection
and yet choose to leave out
the homage stitch
or are we
essentially imperfect
and the purposeful error
only a symbol?

Beth with Hummingbirds

Beth into her lap
hummingbirds dip
small fans ruffle
spin disturb
yellow and green
hummingbirds dip
like a race car no
more like electricity
without the shock
hummingbirds dip
into Beth her lap

Dad Scents

My dad smelled like
old spice and old books
Spinoza, Keats,
Jung and Shakespeare
typewriter ribbon
head and shoulders
vinyl dust on Beethoven records
played on high volume for his one deaf ear
white starched shirts from the cleaners
shaving cream and witch hazel
Nivea lotion and Crest
Gold Bond powder and talc
leather shoes and jacket
creams to grow hair on his bald spot
yellow dog fur
parsley and lemons
red wine, sometimes gin
tonic and limes
reel to reel tape
cherry pipe tobacco
Subaru seats
occasional marijuana
his second wife's perfume
fountain pen ink
chalk and student papers
pigeons on sills
car exhaust as he pulled away
the phone receiver when we talked
alcohol and liniment
chemo and radiation
too little too late
Christmas pine our last time together
incense and the sweet smell of dirt

Second sleep

We find ourselves awake at 3am,
you want to talk about your truck.
Last Monday's accident caved in
the passenger side frame
knocked the bumper right off
a rear-ender for the books.
Thankfully you are not badly hurt
just a sore neck, some stiff muscles.
The guy who hit you with his Lexus
airbags deploying from all sides
walked away apologizing,
his car and your truck totaled.

Now here we are in bed awake
talking about new trucks
or used ones what is the best
way to go and how great
your 2004 Chevy Silverado was,
a rare find in pristine shape
four years ago. What you really
want, I can tell, is your truck back.

There is something conspiratory
about being awake in the dark
in the night together in bed
just sharing thoughts, touching
hands, laughing like long lived
couples have always done.

I bring the computer into bed
where we search for trucks,
the room a web of blue. The
internet world looks strange
against the sheets and pillows.

We rest there awake or almost
until 5 or so. Watch as first light
makes its way through the blinds,
disturbs our intermezzo. So we
close the computer and our eyes
sink into the old world calm
of second sleep.

Elephant Custard

At twelve and nine, my brother and I
walked the few blocks
from our grandparents' house
in Margate, New Jersey to the beach,
home of Lucy the Elephant.
This huge hollow elephant-shaped building
used to be a restaurant and hotel.
A window in her leg sold hot dogs, burgers
and soft ice cream the locals called
custard. As a native New Yorker
my understanding of custard
involved eggs and an oven, but this
was lovely, yellow vanilla (pronounced
vaNElla) or swirls of chocolate in choice
of sugar or wafer cone dripped down
our chins on a good hot day.
We'd run across the long sand beach
feet burning, to the ocean, wash off
the sweet remnants of our nickel indulgence.

Dinner with a Friend

for Corinne

Tonight we told stories about our brothers.
You and yours imagined houses on tracks
that moved with the sun, a great idea if you
don't include the cost or lack of basements.

I recounted how my brother and I
would make recordings long silly stories
complete with songs and sound effects
how we used to laugh and laugh.

Concluding our stories, we took on
fake foreign accents telling jokes our
brothers may or may not remember.
Perhaps this is what it's like to have a sister.

Why My Grandfather Didn't Sell My Mother to the Yiddish Theatre

My mother says my grandfather
often used to tell her
when she sang and danced
at three and four years old
that he would sell her
to the Yiddish Theatre.
However in another
version of the story
they boarded a bus
to somewhere in Philly
where auditions
supposedly were held
but no one was there
and so they went home.
She tells me my grandfather
was planning to join also
which would certainly have been
a surprise to my grandmother,
who had no idea where they went.

Praise to the Earth

Praise to the ocean, waves and foam, bright reef fish hiding in anemone, sharks and whales doze below, above them cormorants and gannets float. To waves that roll into shore at night, the moon reflecting sea foam's white, the breakers in sync with our breathing as the buoy bell sings in the harbor.

Praise to tiny creatures, amoebae and molds, bacteria, to the algae sisters Chloro, Phaeo and Rhodophyta, green and blue-green. lichen, moss and plankton. Praise to nanobes and eukaryotes.

Praise to beach roses, pink under street lights; to peonies, iris and lilac; even at midnight inhale the scent; to the bees, safe in their hive, to evening clouds, white moon behind them; summer rain, watering the gardens.

Praise to writers and scribblers, fruit in the bowl, mat on the table, water in the mug. To the record on the turntable, the hat on the hat stand, the coat on the chair.

Praise to new parents walking a baby, to the restless soldier home from war. Praise to the peacemakers.

To poets, listeners to the night noises, cicadas, clapping of wings. To snorers and dreamers, singers in their sleep. Praise to the Earth, our home.

Cuddling with Mom

Sitting next to you on your bed
in this place you call
such a nice inn
ask *where am I today?*
when am I going home?
You curl your body forward
place your head on my lap
and sleep beneath my hand.

why I will plant a garden this year

to see something green
peeking out of the soil
anything new will do

my mother fell today
she's on blood thinners
and even a bruise can be dangerous

age frightens me
my own white hair
her voice pouring out my mouth

will planting make me young again
new life shooting skyward, flowers
bursting like nurseries of stars

Perhaps Fireflies

sitting here at home
the fat cat purring next to me
all seems well, I hear a neighbor
sneeze, the clang of her new clock
there is a moment to sip coffee

I think of our old cat who died
and the past comes barreling down
or more like little balls
rolling down a hill, no, dancing
in the air like origami boxes

or maybe more like butterflies, no
not insects, certainly not locusts
eating past events
like King's *Langoliers*

and not like fireflies
well, perhaps fireflies
in early summer yards
one then ten then fifty

an image in each flash
my daughters, baby curls,
legs dangling,
then long, crossed,
in heels, teen color

Salt

Nobody puts their children on a boat
unless the water is safer than the land

WARSAN SHIRE

We have forgotten how
our mothers left their fathers' lands
crossed uneven planking
onto vessels of doubt.

Suffered salt water, heat
and loneliness
in bruised pursuit
of promises

cultivated like seeds beneath
sore and weathered feet
calloused on that long walk
from shore to shore.

They believed the sea
would heal them
from ravages of war
or deluge of hunger.

We their children
ignore the documents
forged in congresses
argued in assemblies

call new immigrants
rapists and *job-stealers*
make them flee to other lands
despite their families waiting

like our mothers' mothers
waited to take their daughters
in their arms
to hold them again.

Instead, children's bodies
wash up on a Turkish beach
a family rejected
by mounds of Canadian red tape.

Tether

The world
has shrunk
to the size
of my mother
her worry
has me tethered
and I cannot
travel far.
In a dream
thread
stretches
from sky
to ground
enters
the crown
of my head
holding me
down.

Words are Not Enough

Some days I realize
that all I have is words
which are not enough

though I also have
this body to push with
its muscles and sinew

the bit of strength in them
and there is also music
the sound of rain on canvas

the roiling of waves
my feet lead me to dunes
or over stone bridges

and the smell of moss,
lavender, or grape iris
and the taste of roses

fog or salt in the wind
creak of tree sap
wails of nesting crows

orange hills at dusk
then indigo evening
and limitless starlight

which is
more than I can fathom
or just enough.

LORI DESROSIERS' other poetry books are *The Philosopher's Daughter*, Salmon Poetry, 2013, and *Sometimes I Hear the Clock Speak*, Salmon Poetry, 2016. She has two chapbooks, *Inner Sky* (2015) and *typing with e.e. cummings* (2019), both from Glass Lyre Press. Her poems have appeared in *New Millennium Review, Cutthroat, Peacock Journal, String Poet, Blue Fifth Review, Pirene's Fountain, New Verse News, Mom Egg Review*, and many other journals and anthologies. She was a finalist for the Joy Harjo poetry contest and the New Millennium contest. Her poem "about the body" won the Liakoura poetry award from Glass Lyre Press. She holds an MFA in Poetry from New England College. Her work has been nominated for a Pushcart Prize. She founded and edits *Naugatuck River Review*, a journal of narrative poetry and Wordpeace.co, an online journal dedicated to social justice. She teaches Poetry in the Interdisciplinary Studies program for the Lesley University M.F.A. graduate program. Her website is loridesrosierspoetry.com.

salmonpoetry

Cliffs of Moher, County Clare, Ireland

"Like the sea-run Steelhead salmon that
thrashes upstream to its spawning ground,
then instead of dying, returns to the sea—
Salmon Poetry Press brings precious cargo to
both Ireland and America in the poetry it
publishes, then carries that select work to its
readership against incalculable odds."

TESS GALLAGHER

The Salmon Bookshop & Literary Centre

Ennistymon, County Clare, Ireland

"Another wonderful Clare outlet."
The Irish Times, 35 Best Independent Bookshops